I0483337

period.

JEANNE CRISCOLA

Useless press

FOR ONLINE INFORMATION AND ORDERING OF THIS
AND OTHER USELESS BOOKS, PLEASE VISIT
WWW.USELESSPRESS.COM.

FOR MORE INFORMATION, PLEASE CONTACT
USELESS PRESS
1477 RIDGE ROAD
NORTH HAVEN, CT 06473
EMAIL: INFO@USELESSPRESS.COM

©2016 BY USELESS PRESS + JEANNE CRISCOLA

ALL RIGHTS RESERVED.

NO PART OF THIS PUBLICATION MAY BE
REPRODUCED, STORED IN A RETRIEVAL SYSTEM,
OR TRANSMITTED, IN ANY FORM OR BY MEANS
ELECTRONIC, MECHANICAL, PHOTOCOPYING, OR
OTHERWISE, WITHOUT PRIOR WRITTEN PERMISSION
OF THE PRESS.

CONCEPT, DESIGN, TYPE: JEANNE CRISCOLA

ISBN: 978-0-692-64305-1

FOR FAMILY CRESER

Rock

Olivia

and Frank

●

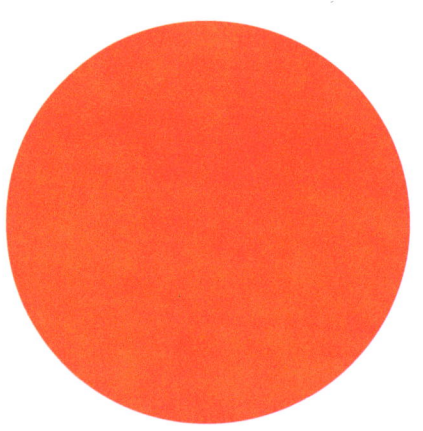

100

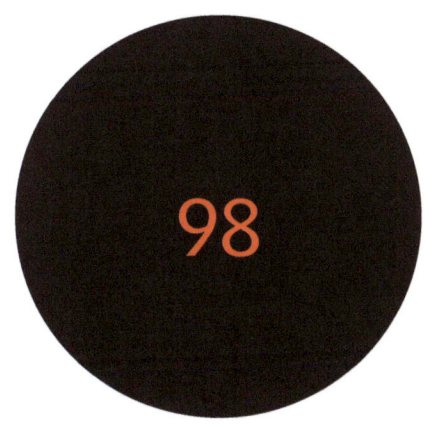

98

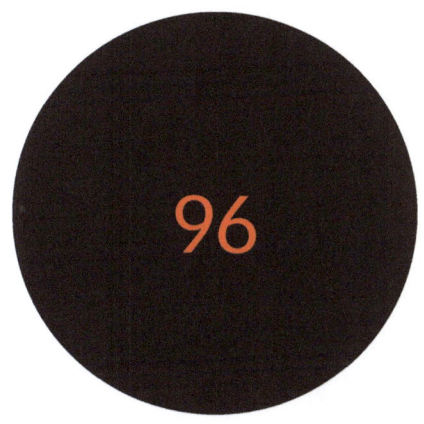

96

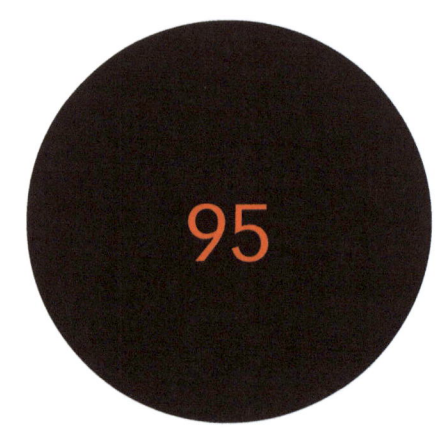

95

94

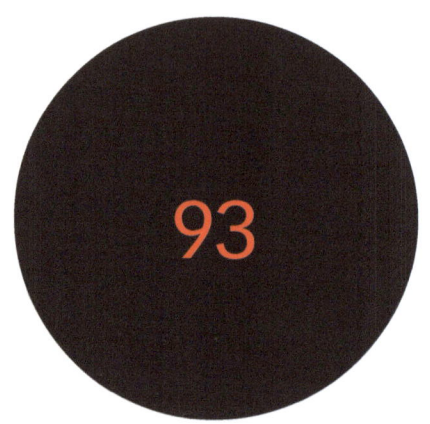

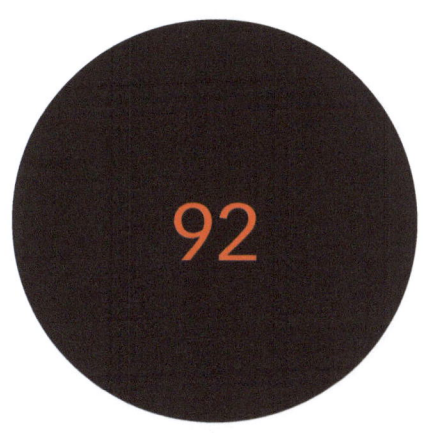

91

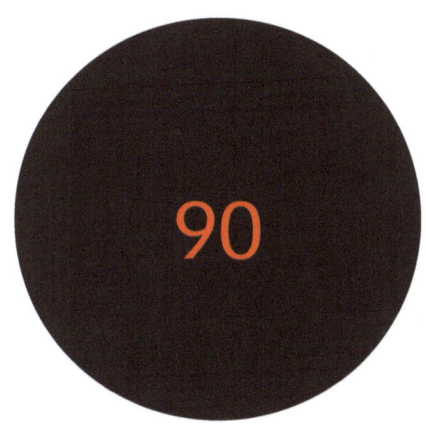

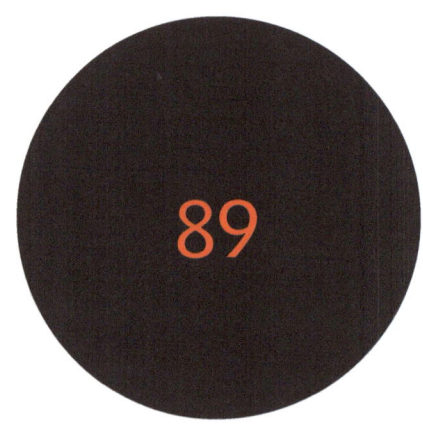

89

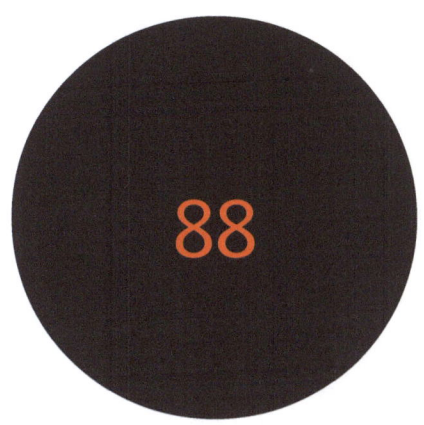

88

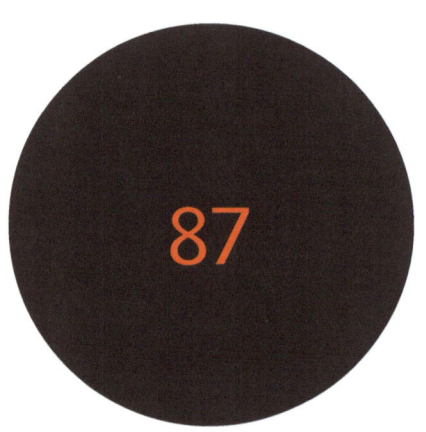

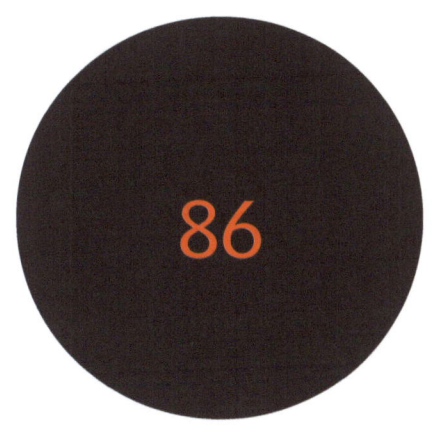

86

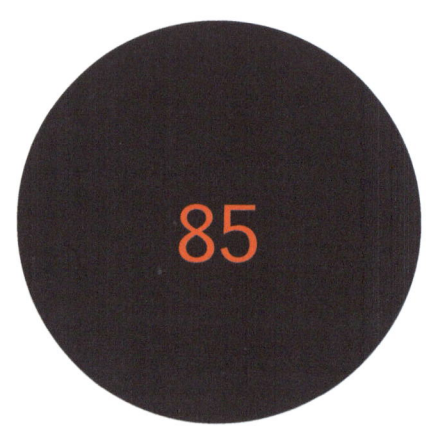

85

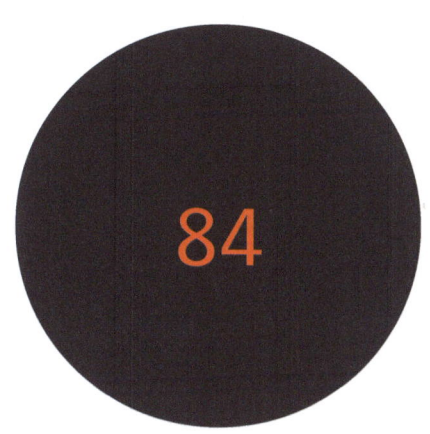

84

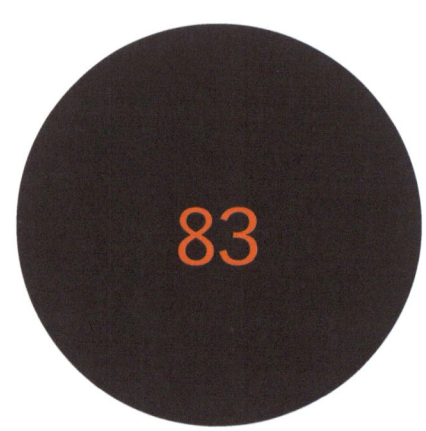

83

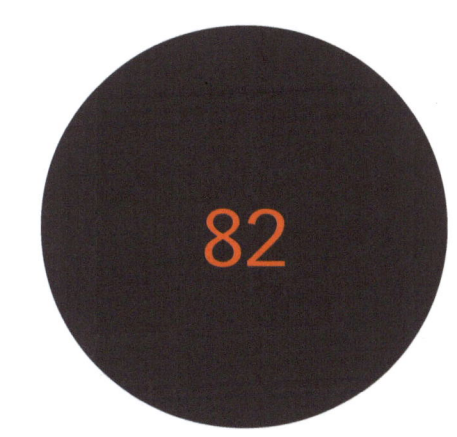

82

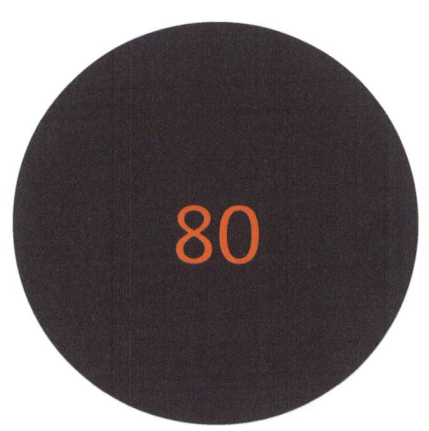

80

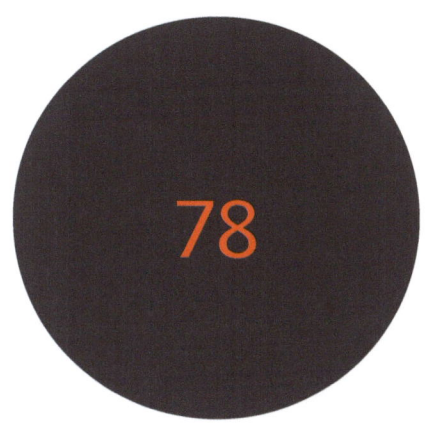

78

77

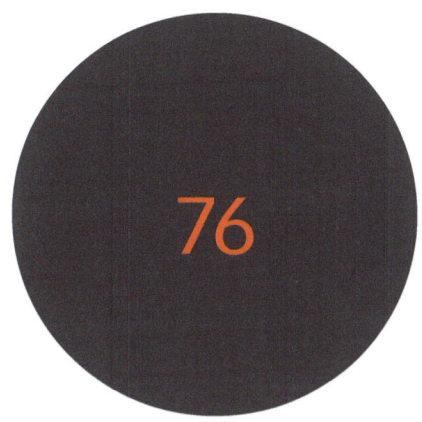

76

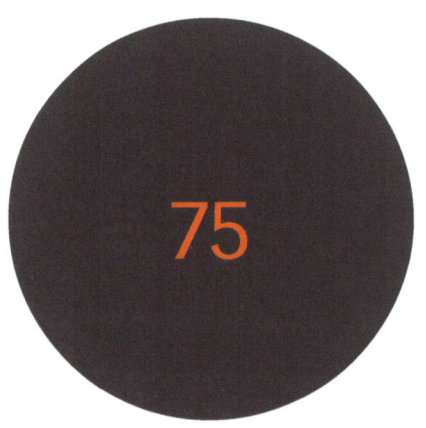

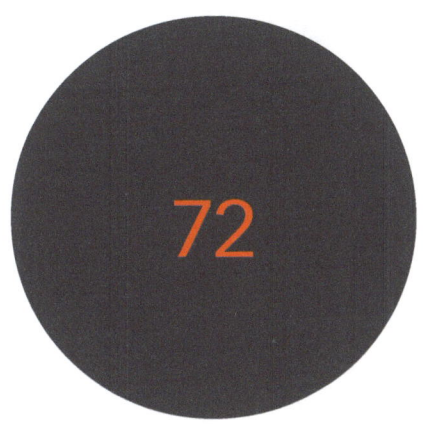

72

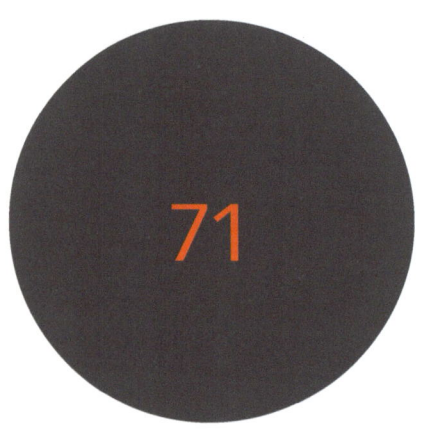

71

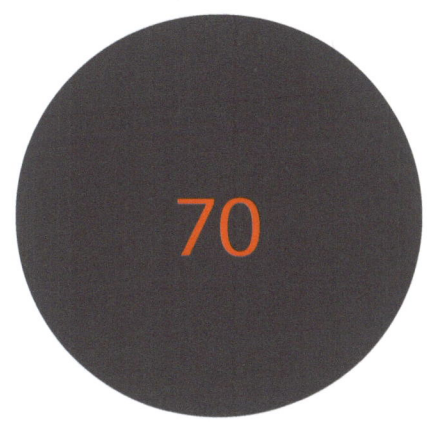

70

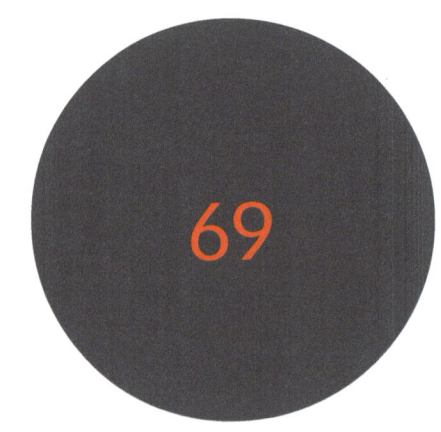

69

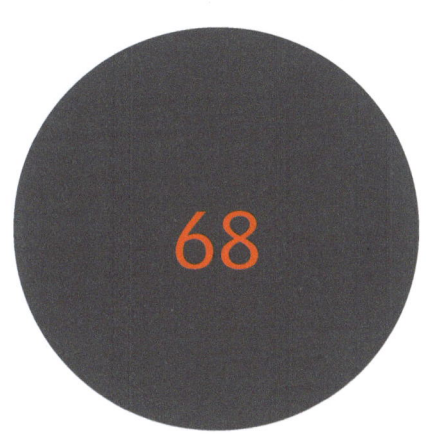

68

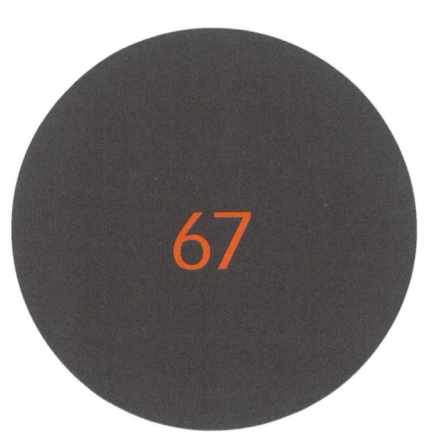

67

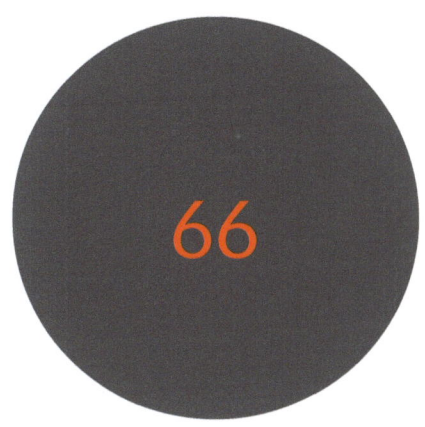

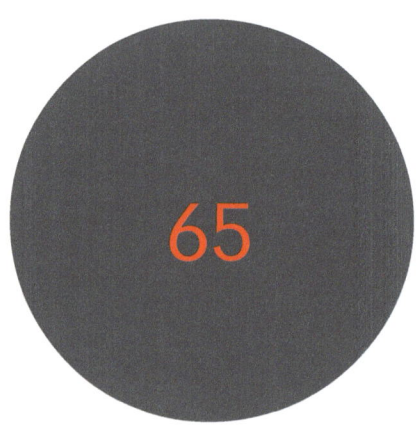

65

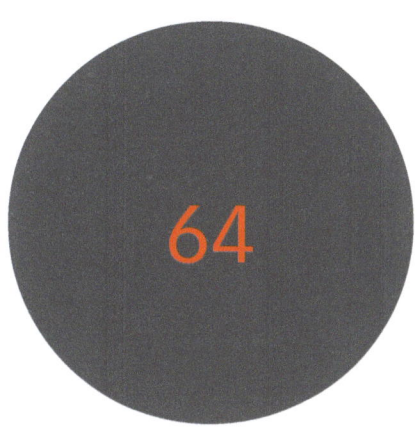

64

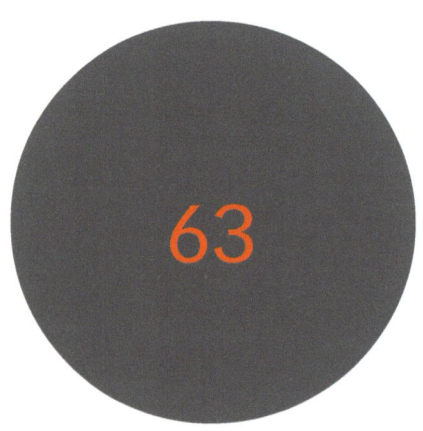

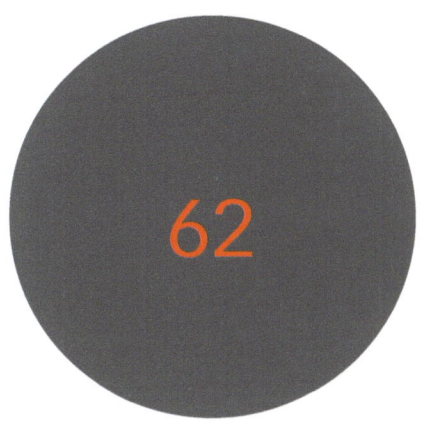

62

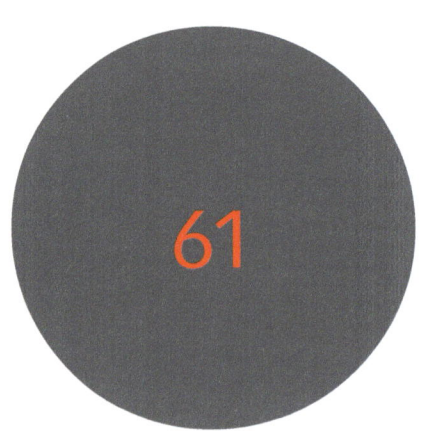

61

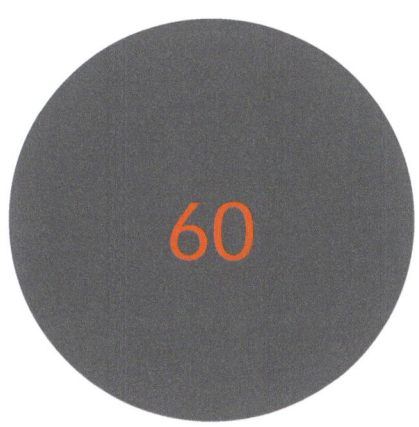

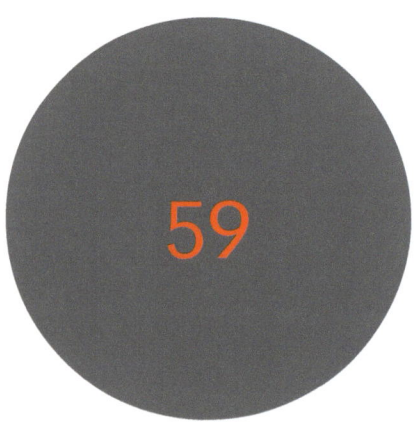

59

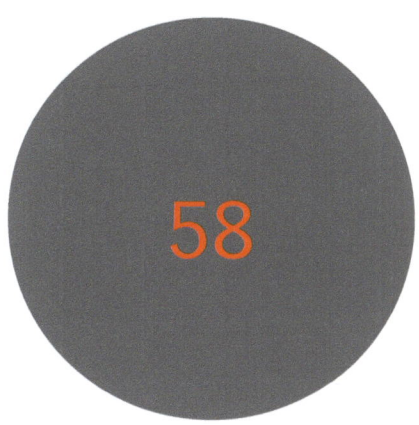

58

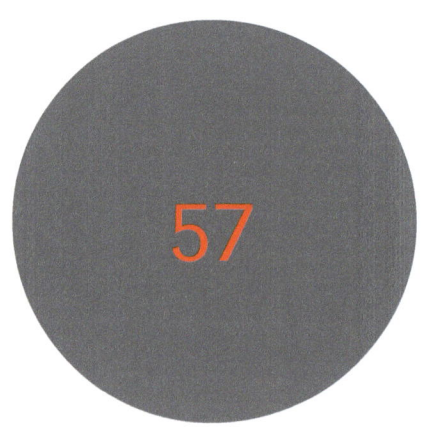

57

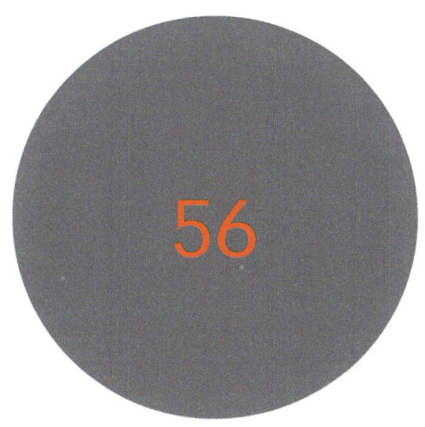

56

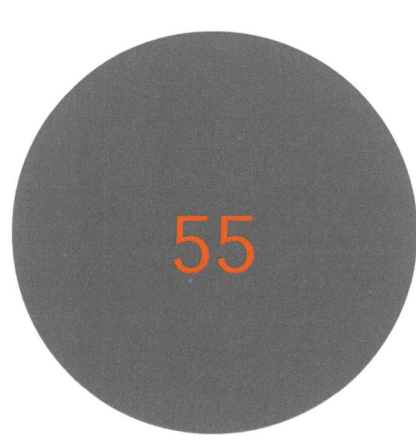

55

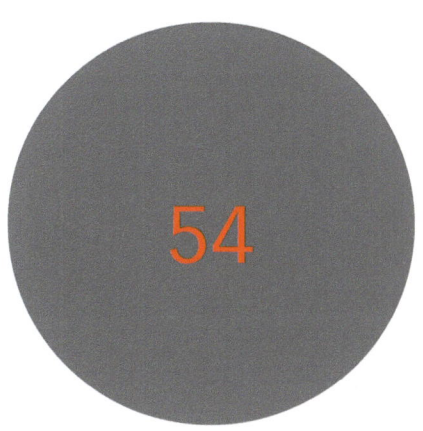

54

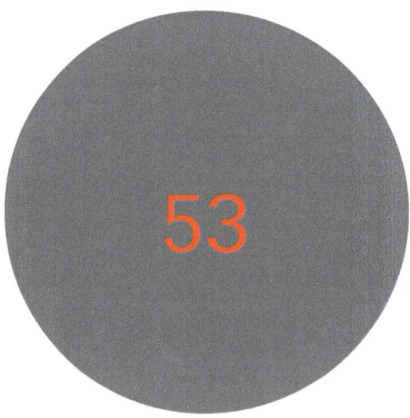

53

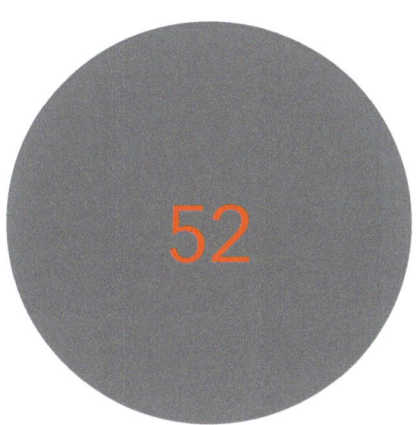

52

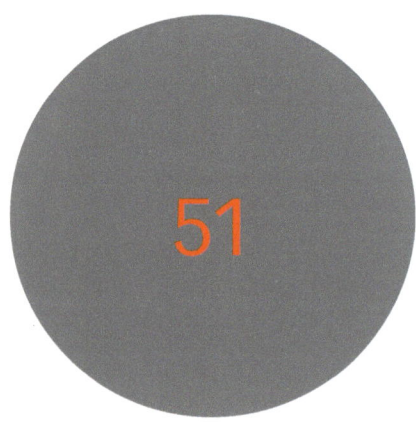

51

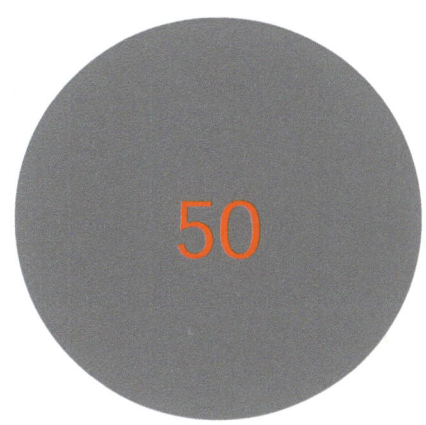

50

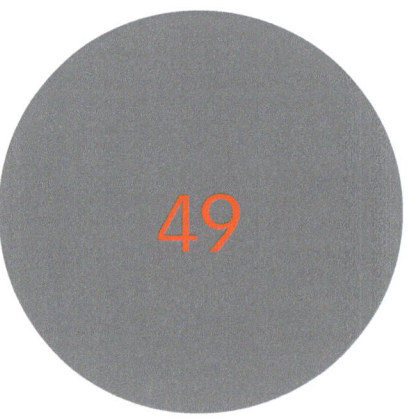

49

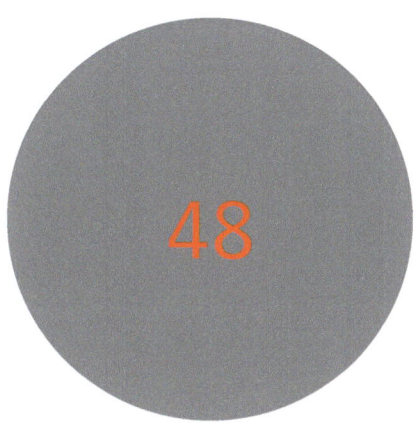

48

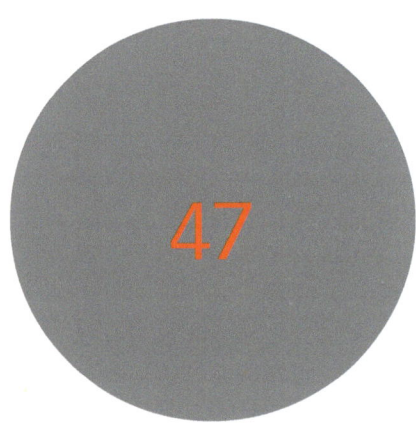

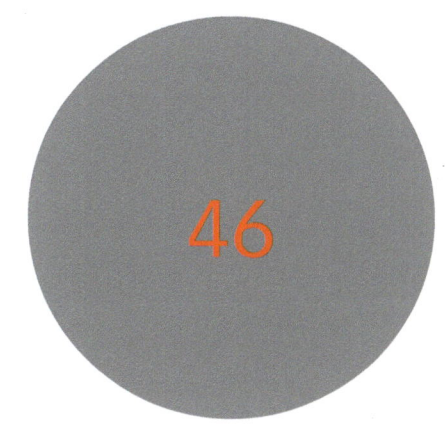

46

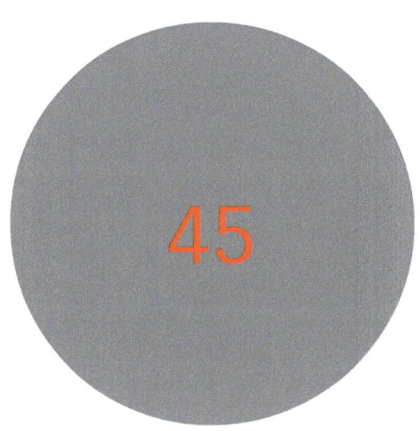

45

44

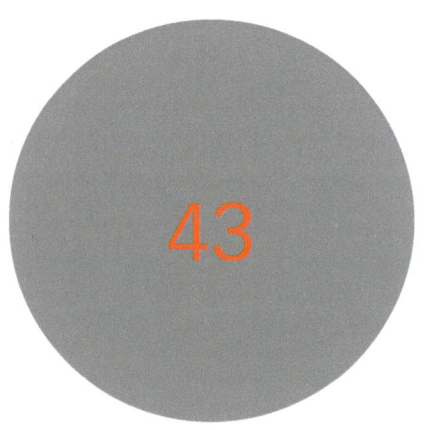

43

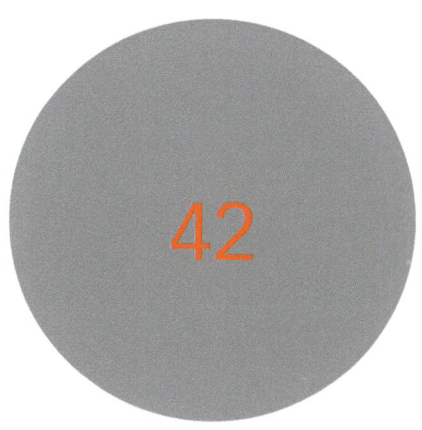

41

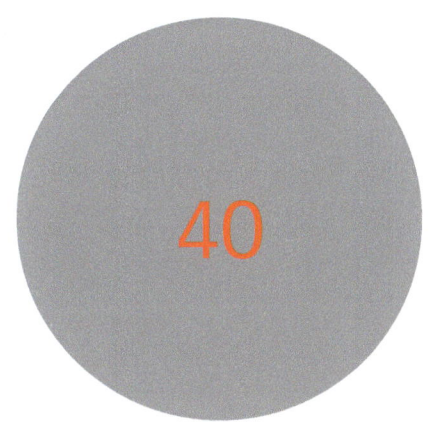

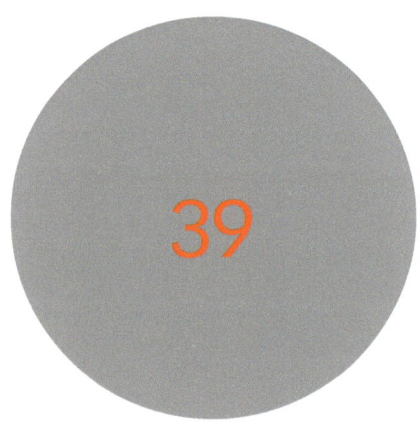

39

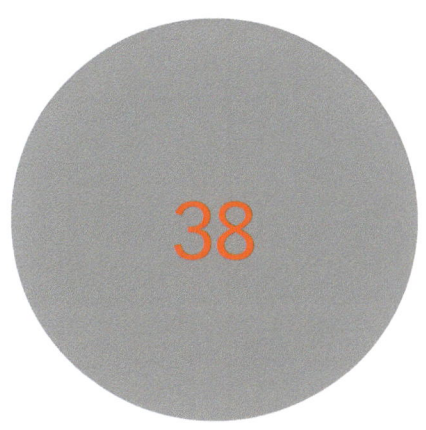

38

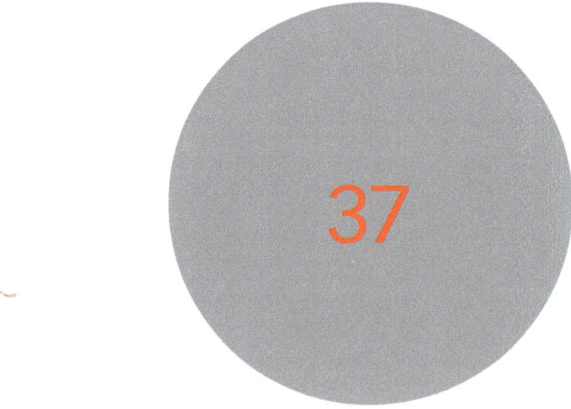

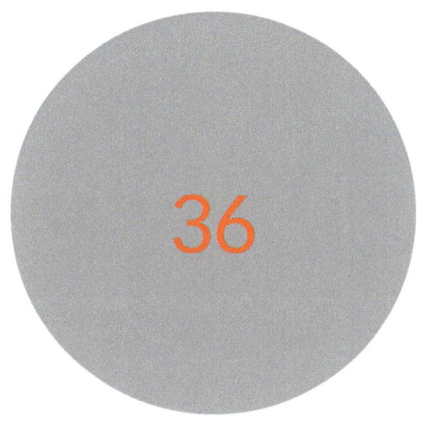

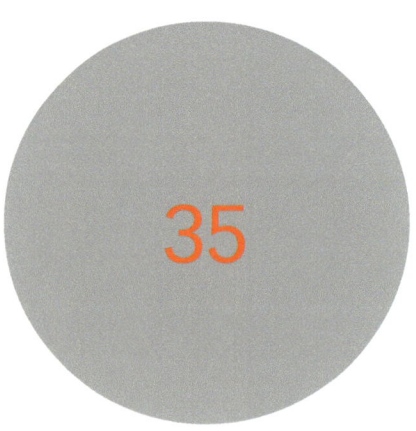

34

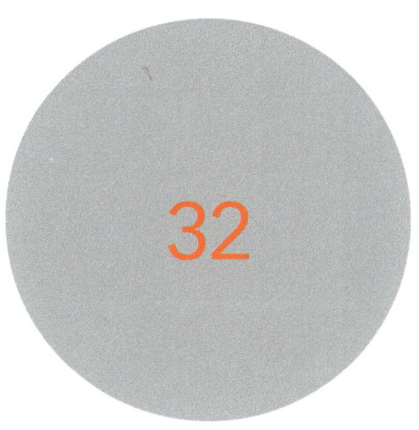

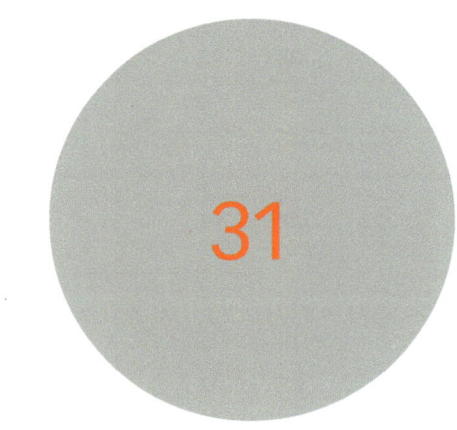

31

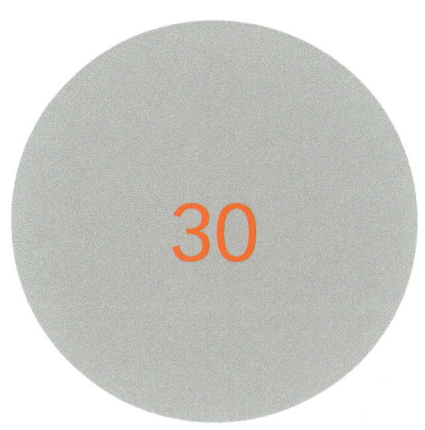

30

29

28

27

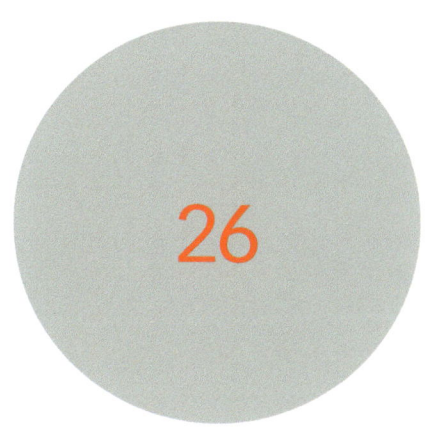

26

23

22

21

20

16

15

13

12

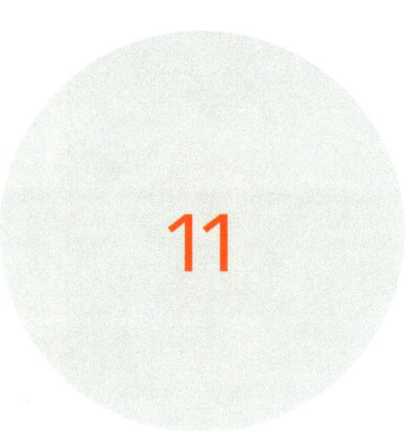

11

10

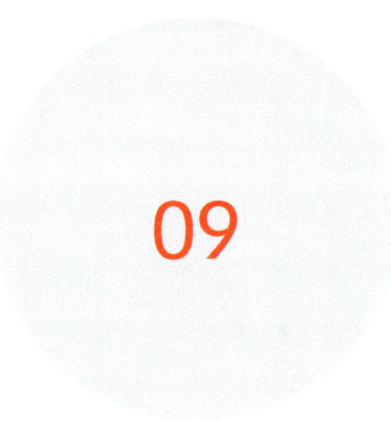

09

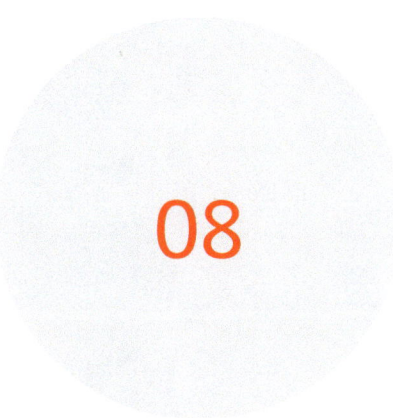

08

07

06

05

04

03

02

01

00

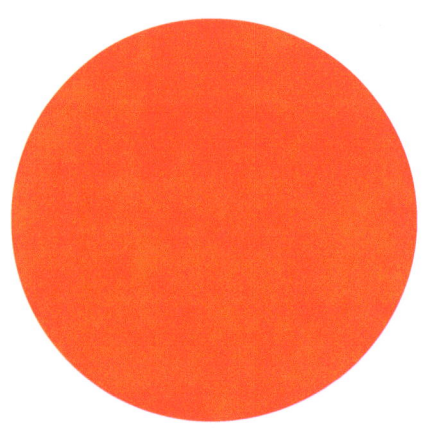

www.ingramcontent.com/pod-product-compliance
Lightning Source LLC
Chambersburg PA
CBHW041239200526
45159CB00032B/2628